MIDDLE SCHOOL
Motivators!

*22 Interactive
Learning Structures*

Responsive Classroom®
MIDDLE SCHOOL

ISBN: 978-1-892989-82-6
Library of Congress Control Number: 2015954153

Photographs by Jeff Woodward
Silhouettes © Lynn Zimmerman, Lucky Dog Designs

Center for Responsive Schools wishes to thank the many people whose hard work and dedication to students and educators have made this book possible. Special thanks go to middle school educators Christine Diaz and Rio Clemente for their careful reading of and feedback on the manuscript.

Center for Responsive Schools, Inc.
85 Avenue A, P.O. Box 718
Turners Falls, MA 01376-0718

800-360-6332
www.responsiveclassroom.org

CONTENTS

A Win-Win for You and Your Students

| **Your students** want to move, socialize, have fun. | **You** want them to fully engage with the content you're teaching. |

How can you meet their goals—and yours—while keeping behavior positive and building classroom community?

Interactive learning structures to the rescue!

Getting Started

Middle school motivators are interactive learning structures—easy-to-use activities like Swap Meet (p. 18) that has students pairing up with various classmates to exchange ideas for solving a problem or Venn-ting (p. 20) in which students analyze similarities and differences by creating a Venn diagram with partners or in small groups. By giving students opportunities to move around a bit, positively interact with peers, and stretch their thinking, these interactive learning structures motivate students to engage more deeply with their learning.

What's more, these structures enable you to provide varied opportunities for lively learning while maintaining order and purposefulness in your classroom. Each structure helps you quickly organize students into pairs or small groups and provides a format that helps students work together on a specific learning goal, assignment, or project. And these structures promote positive behavior by meeting young adolescents' developmental need for learning that's both active (hands-on, experiential) and interactive (social, collaborative).

Going Beyond Mere Fun and Games

Interactive learning structures are fun, but they're much more than that. They are also ignitors of learning. By piquing students' interest in the material, these structures encourage maximum effort and strengthen students' academic and social-emotional skills. By letting students interact in positive ways with classmates, these structures help build a positive classroom community. And by giving you quick and easy ways to organize students' learning, they help you make the most of your most valuable and limited resource—time. The result: improved motivation and learning outcomes for every student you teach. (See facing page for a list of benefits.)

Using Interactive Learning Structures Effectively

The following tips will help you get the most out of the 22 structures in this book:

Take time to plan and reflect

To help students be successful, it's important to give yourself time to plan how you'll use each structure. Think about the learning goal, whether your classroom allows enough space for the structure you have in mind, and if students are developmentally ready to do it—for example, can they exercise self-control when everyone's moving around the room at the same time? Then after students have used the structure, take some time to reflect on what went well and what didn't, and adjust as needed next time.

Benefits of Using Interactive Learning Structures

Building Students' Skills

Because interactive learning structures make learning lively and engaging, they help students build:

Academic Learning Skills

* **Academic Mindset:** Belief that abilities are not fixed, but grow with effort.

* **Academic Perseverance:** Willingness to keep working hard, even when facing challenges.

* **Academic Behaviors:** Actions that demonstrate taking responsibility for one's learning (such as coming to class ready to listen, work, and participate).

* **Learning Strategies:** Study skills and higher-level thinking skills that students consciously use to understand content and achieve learning goals.

Social-Emotional Learning Skills

* **Cooperation:** Working productively and collaboratively with others.

* **Assertiveness:** Taking individual initiative and developing positive self-identity.

* **Responsibility:** Motivating oneself to work hard and choose positive courses of action.

* **Empathy:** Understanding and appreciating another person's ideas, beliefs, and feelings.

* **Self-Control:** Recognizing and regulating one's own thoughts, emotions, and behaviors.

Boosting Teacher Effectiveness

By using these structures, you'll find that you're better able to:

* Pique students' interest in the content.

* Motivate students to maximize effort.

* Help students develop leadership and teamwork skills.

* Reduce off-task behaviors.

* Provide safe, productive peer-to-peer interactions.

* Build a positive classroom community.

* Make the most of limited classroom time.

3

Make sure students have the skills they need

You'll want to make sure that any structure you choose is relatively easy for all students to use successfully so it supports rather than interferes with learning goals. For example, Maître d' (page 40) requires students to move around the classroom to form small groups with different classmates and share a wide range of ideas, so you'd want to be sure they can do both of those things successfully. One quick, effective way to teach skills like these is by using a *Responsive Classroom* practice called Interactive Modeling. Here's how you might use this four-step practice to teach students safe movement:

1 **Describe and explain what you'll model.** Your brief statement helps students focus: "We're going to share ideas by doing a cool learning activity called Maître d'. We'll move around the classroom a lot, so I'll first demonstrate what safe movement looks like."

2 **Model while students notice.** Don't narrate as you demonstrate the skill or routine; instead, let students concentrate on observing the key aspects themselves. Afterward, ask them what they noticed.

3 **Give students the opportunity to collaborate and practice.** Immediate practice helps students get the steps down while your demonstration is fresh in their minds.

4 **Reinforce their practice with immediate feedback.** Name students' specific, positive actions and respectfully correct mistakes to solidify their understanding: "You all took care in moving throughout the room quietly and safely when forming groups."

Use pairs as the starting point

Working with just one person can feel safer for students as they develop their academic conversation skills, so have students start working in pairs rather than small groups or as a whole class. Use the "At a Glance" charts on pages 8–11 to find structures that will help students work effectively in pairs.

Form pairs and groups purposefully

Most of the structures in this book call for putting students in pairs or small groups of three or four. Think about the learning goal, as well as students' abilities and interests, when assigning them to pairs or groups. Some ways to form groups are mixed abilities, mixed interests, similar abilities, similar interests, or randomly. When you think students are ready to be respectful and inclusive, give them some autonomy in choosing their own partners or groupmates.

Speak briefly, directly, and genuinely

Because a teacher's language—words, tone, and pace—is one of the most powerful teaching tools available, how you speak to the class while using these structures helps ensure their success. Effective teacher language helps students learn by conveying faith in their abilities and intentions, and by focusing on their actions rather than their character or personality. Throughout this book, you'll see examples of teacher language that supports students' learning, including:

* Open-ended questions—to draw on middle schoolers' thoughts, knowledge, skills, experiences, and feelings and to acknowledge their eagerness to share their ideas: "What do you already know about how the liver works and why it's essential to good health?"

* Reinforcing language—to identify and affirm students' positive actions and accomplishments, which helps them continue to learn and grow: "You made sure each person had an equal chance to talk." "You backed up your ideas with evidence."

* Reminding language—to prompt students to remember for themselves the expectations you've taught: "What's one thing you can do if your group gets stuck on a challenge?"

State the expectations for small group learning

It's important to emphasize that you expect everyone to make a contribution and that both individual and group effort determine success. Regularly remind students of these expectations whenever they're about to begin working with partners or in small groups.

Clarify roles and responsibilities

To ensure true collaboration, teach students how to carry out their individual roles and responsibilities as members of a group or team. Often you'll want to assign specific roles within each group, such as:

* Facilitator—keeps the group focused on their collaborative task and makes sure all voices are heard

* Recorder (note taker)—takes notes for the group

* Reporter—collects ideas from other groups and reports them back to their own group

* Presenter—shares out the group's ideas

Be specific when teaching each of these roles: name exactly what to do and model as needed. Post anchor charts that list roles and responsibilities to support students in being successful.

Giving Clear Directions

When using any interactive learning structure, students benefit from clear, sequential directions. Besides giving verbal directions, you might want to post them on a chart or board for students to refer to as needed.

In the following example, the teacher uses Debate Duos (p. 12) to help students gain new perspectives by taking both the "for" and the "against" sides of an argument. Notice how concise and focused the teacher's instructions are.

1. **Name the task (or learning goal).** "You'll use what you've learned about energy needs and environmental protection to debate this question with your assigned partner: 'Should we drill for oil and gas in protected parks and reserves?'"

2. **Name roles and responsibilities.** "Position A is 'Yes, drill.' Position B is 'No, don't drill.' The partner taking Position A will have 30 seconds to speak. Then the Position B partner will have 30 seconds to speak."

3. **Explain timing and transitions.** "You'll have three minutes total. Every 30 seconds, I'll call out 'Switch.' The person listening then speaks. When I ring the chime, this round of the debate ends. Then you'll switch positions and find a new partner."

4. **Ask if there are any questions.** "Any questions?"

5. **Release students to work.** "OK, get started."

Ready, Set, Enjoy

The best way to get started using interactive learning structures is to dive right in. Check the "At a Glance" charts that follow to choose a structure by grouping (pairs, small groups, whole class). Then scan the "Often Used For" column to find one that suits your purpose. To help you quickly and efficiently teach each structure, you'll find:

* Clear, easy-to-follow instructions

* Sample reminding and reinforcing language

* Sample topics and questions to help focus students' discussions

* "In Action" scenarios showing a class using the structure

And for several structures that ask students to jot down key facts or ideas, you'll also find note-taking handouts on pages 56–67. Feel free to copy and use these as is or adapt them to fit your needs.

You'll soon see how these interactive learning structures bring any content alive—motivating students to engage enthusiastically and purposefully with the material and with each other, to understand content more deeply, and to remember more of what they've learned.

At a Glance—Interactive Learning Structures

PAIRS

STRUCTURE	OFTEN USED FOR	SKILLS PRACTICED	PAGE
Debate Duos (also for small groups)	Evaluating content; developing skills for crafting an argument; understanding multiple perspectives; analyzing information	Agreeing and disagreeing respectfully; making inferences; reasoning; strategizing	**12**
Inside-Outside Circles/Parallel Lines	Previewing or reviewing content; developing skills for crafting an argument; reflecting on content or process	Reasoning; staying focused; summarizing; voicing an opinion	**14**
Quiz Trade	Preparing for test-taking; recalling information; assessing understanding	Brainstorming; reasoning; summarizing; synthesizing	**16**
Swap Meet	Exploring different strategies for solving problems; deepening understanding; analyzing multiple perspectives	Brainstorming; reasoning; staying focused; summarizing	**18**
Venn-ting (also for small groups)	Comparing and contrasting; identifying main ideas; reviewing content	Agreeing and disagreeing respectfully; brainstorming; summarizing; synthesizing	**20**
Walk and Talk	Re-energizing and refocusing attention; exploring ideas and perspectives; understanding multiple perspectives	Exchanging ideas; reasoning; staying on topic; summarizing; voicing an opinion	**22**
Word Splash (also for small groups and whole class)	Accessing background knowledge; recalling information; previewing or reviewing content	Creative thinking; making inferences; public speaking; summarizing; synthesizing	**24**

SMALL GROUPS

STRUCTURE	OFTEN USED FOR	SKILLS PRACTICED	PAGE
Amazing Analogies (also for pairs)	Comparing and contrasting; deepening understanding; bringing closure to a lesson or topic	Brainstorming; creative thinking; giving meaningful feedback; synthesizing	26
Around-the-Clock	Analyzing information; developing skills for crafting an argument; identifying main ideas	Asking and answering questions thoughtfully; distinguishing fact from opinion; reasoning; strategizing	28
Beat the Clock (also for pairs)	Recalling information; deepening understanding; reviewing content	Brainstorming; strategizing; summarizing; synthesizing	30
Consensus Mapping	Identifying main ideas; finding consensus; developing skills for crafting an argument	Agreeing and disagreeing respectfully; persuading others; reasoning; strategizing	32
Four Corners (also for pairs)	Previewing or reviewing content; developing skills for crafting an argument; understanding multiple perspectives	Agreeing and disagreeing respectfully; reasoning; voicing an opinion	34
Jigsaws	Developing and sharing expertise on a topic or issue; processing content in smaller chunks; analyzing multiple perspectives	Exchanging ideas; staying on topic; summarizing; synthesizing	36
The Last Word (also for whole class)	Recalling information; identifying main ideas; reviewing content	Brainstorming; creative thinking; public speaking; summarizing; synthesizing	38
Maître d'	Previewing or reviewing content; developing skills for crafting an argument; understanding multiple perspectives	Reasoning; staying focused; voicing an opinion	40
One-Sentence/ One-Word Summaries (also for whole class)	Identifying main ideas; bringing closure to a lesson or topic; reviewing content	Public speaking; reasoning; summarizing; synthesizing	42

CONTINUED ▶

STRUCTURE	OFTEN USED FOR	SKILLS PRACTICED	PAGE
Say Something (also for pairs)	Processing content in smaller chunks; identifying main ideas; understanding multiple perspectives	Asking and answering questions thoughtfully; summarizing; synthesizing	44
Stay and Stray	Exploring different strategies for solving problems; developing skills for crafting an argument; analyzing multiple perspectives	Asking and answering questions thoughtfully; giving meaningful feedback; reasoning; summarizing; synthesizing	46
World Café*	Understanding multiple perspectives; developing skills for crafting an argument; reviewing content	Agreeing and disagreeing respectfully; reasoning; staying focused; voicing an opinion	48

*World Café™ is a registered trademark of World Café Community Foundation, Greenbrae, CA, www.theworldcafe.com.

WHOLE CLASS

STRUCTURE	OFTEN USED FOR	SKILLS PRACTICED	PAGE
Fact or Fiction (also for small groups)	Distinguishing fact from fiction; assessing understanding; previewing or reviewing content	Brainstorming; creative thinking; making inferences; public speaking; summarizing	50
Shared Truths (also for small groups)	Comparing and contrasting; previewing or reviewing content; analyzing multiple perspectives	Brainstorming; creative thinking; making inferences; public speaking	52
Snowball	Bringing closure to a lesson or topic; understanding multiple perspectives; reflecting on content or process	Public speaking; reasoning; summarizing; voicing an opinion	54

ALPHABETICAL ORDER

STRUCTURE	GROUPING	PAGE
Amazing Analogies	small groups (also pairs)	26
Around-the-Clock	small groups	28
Beat the Clock	small groups (also pairs)	30
Consensus Mapping	small groups	32
Debate Duos	pairs (also small groups)	12
Fact or Fiction	whole class (also small groups)	50
Four Corners	small groups (also pairs)	34
Inside-Outside Circles/Parallel Lines	pairs	14
Jigsaws	small groups	36
The Last Word	small groups (also whole class)	38
Maître d'	small groups	40
One-Sentence/One-Word Summaries	small groups (also whole class)	42
Quiz Trade	pairs	16
Say Something	small groups (also pairs)	44
Shared Truths	whole class (also small groups)	52
Snowball	whole class	54
Stay and Stray	small groups	46
Swap Meet	pairs	18
Venn-ting	pairs (also small groups)	20
Walk and Talk	pairs	22
Word Splash	pairs (also small groups/whole class)	24
World Café	small groups	48

Pairs

Debate Duos

In Brief

In pairs, students debate two sides of an argument to consider various perspectives.

*

Skills Practiced

Agreeing and disagreeing respectfully

Making inferences

Reasoning

Strategizing

*

Time Frame

10–15 minutes

*

Materials

Debate Duos worksheet (p. 58)

Timer

*

Variation

Students work in groups of four: Two students take position A and two take position B.

1. **Name the learning goal.** For example: "You're going to use what you've learned about economics to debate the minimum wage." Then frame the issue for the debate: "Should the minimum wage in our state be raised?"

2. **Teach strategies** (or review as needed) to stay focused, maintain self-control, and strengthen debate skills such as listening attentively, waiting for one's turn to speak, and speaking clearly: "How do you disagree respectfully?"

3. **Pair students and assign roles** (position A, position B). Position A takes the "for" or "pro" side and position B the "against" or "con" side.

4. **Give students 3–5 minutes** to prepare reasons and evidence to support their position on their Debate Duos worksheet (see p. 58). Check in with students and coach them as needed.

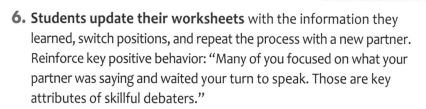

5. **Position A begins** and has 30 uninterrupted seconds to speak for their side. Then position B has 30 uninterrupted seconds to present their side. They take turns supporting their position two or more times, as time allows.

6. **Students update their worksheets** with the information they learned, switch positions, and repeat the process with a new partner. Reinforce key positive behavior: "Many of you focused on what your partner was saying and waited your turn to speak. Those are key attributes of skillful debaters."

Debate Duos in Action

The performing arts teacher uses Debate Duos to help students gain a deeper appreciation of stage acting and screen acting. She pairs students and assigns them a position (A or B).

Then the teacher gives clear directions to set students up for success. She first states the learning goal: "With partners, you're going to debate which version of Romeo and Juliet has stronger acting—the play we attended or the film we saw."

Next she explains everyone's roles and the timing: "Position A will argue for the play and position B for the film. Position A has 30 seconds to talk. Then position B will have 30 seconds. You'll go back and forth like this once more. Then find a new partner and debate the opposite position. I'll ring the chime for each transition."

After checking to see if anyone has questions, the teacher signals students to start their debates by ringing the chime. As students debate, she observes and coaches. To conclude the activity, she asks students to consider how they can use the ideas they shared to strengthen their acting skills during play rehearsals later that week.

Learning Goal Examples

Advisory

"Are standardized tests overemphasized in schools?"

English Language Arts and Science

"Could there be life on Mars?"

Health/PE

"Should physical education be offered every day?"

Math and Social Studies

"The penny should be removed from U.S. currency."

Inside-Outside Circles/ Parallel Lines

In Brief

Students have quick, one-on-one conversations with several partners to exchange ideas in response to a question or topic the teacher poses.

∗

Skills Practiced

Reasoning

Staying focused

Summarizing

Voicing an opinion

∗

Time Frame

8–12 minutes (3 or 4 rounds)

∗

Materials

None

∗

Variation

Students make up their own questions or topics for each round.

HOW TO DO IT

1. **Name the learning goal.** For example: "You're going to form an inner and an outer circle [or two parallel lines] to exchange ideas about the essay you'll be writing on the Great Depression."

2. **Have students count off by twos.** Ones form an inner circle facing out, and twos form an outer circle facing in. (Or, students form two lines facing each other.) Each two should be facing a one, forming a pair.

3. **State a question or topic for discussion:** "What's your plan for conducting research about people's lives during the Great Depression?" Give students some think time.

4. **Partners take turns speaking, briefly exchanging ideas.** Allow no more than 1–2 minutes total for this back-and-forth.

5. **Students in the outside circle move one person to the left** to form new pairs. (Or, students in one line move up one person with the first person in line moving to the end of the line.) Remind students about safe movement: "How might you stay in your personal space when moving in your circle [or line]?"

6. **New partners discuss the same question or topic, or a new one that you pose.** Repeat as time allows. Reinforce positive behavior: "I noticed your transitions were quick and efficient. You held productive discussions with each of your partners."

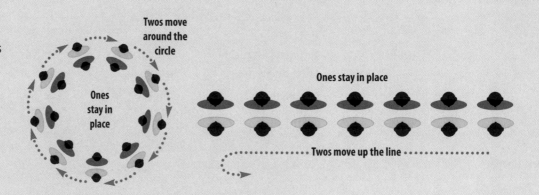

Inside-Outside Circles in Action

A 7th grade math teacher uses Inside-Outside Circles to help students share problem-solving ideas for finding the value of *x* in different types of equations before they take their end-of-unit exam. She gives clear directions to set students up for success.

First she states the learning goal: "In this activity, you'll review for the upcoming math test."

Next she explains everyone's roles and the timing: "At the beginning of each round, I'll give you a new equation to problem-solve with your partner for two minutes. When you hear the chime, wrap up your conversation. Then those in the outside circle will move one spot to the left and form a new partnership."

The teacher checks to see if anyone has questions and then gives students the first problem to solve. After the final round, she highlights specific strategies and clarifies misunderstandings to help students prepare for the exam.

─────────────── **Learning Goal Examples** ───────────────

English Language Arts	**Health/PE**	**Math**	**Science**
"Which scenes demonstrate 'determination' in the book *A Long Walk to Water* by Linda Sue Park? How?"	"What do you think makes a valuable team player, and why?"	"How might carpenters use math in their profession? What about plumbers? Electricians?"	"How do glaciers change the land? Do you think we should do more to preserve glaciers? Why or why not?"

Pairs

In Brief

Students quiz each other as a quick way to review content (such as vocabulary or key ideas) and self-assess how much they know about a topic.

*

Skills Practiced

Brainstorming

Reasoning

Summarizing

Synthesizing

*

Time Frame

10–15 minutes

*

Materials

Index cards or Quiz Trade template (p. 61)

Pencils

Timer

*

Variation

Have students write true/false statements or multiple choice questions with the correct answer and the reason(s) for it on the back.

Quiz Trade

H O W   T O   D O   I T

1. **Name the learning goal.** For example: "You're going to quiz each other on what you've learned about Internet research."

2. **Give each student a Quiz Trade template** (see p. 61). Ask them to think of three main ideas about the topic and write these as Q&As—questions on the front and answers on the back. Allow 3–5 minutes or have students do this in advance. (Students may refer to their textbooks if needed.) A Q&A might be: (Front) "What's one strategy you might try when using a search engine, and why?" (Back) "Check the domain names of the URLs to find reputable sites."

3. **Remind students** about effective communication skills: "How can you phrase your questions so that they're clear and concise?"

4. **Have students walk around the room to find a partner.** (If needed, model how to roam the room safely.) Partner A reads one question, and the two take turns discussing it. Next Partner B reads one question, and again they take turns discussing it. Allow 1–2 minutes for each discussion, giving 15-second warnings.

5. **When time is up, partners swap cards and find new partners.** Repeat until students have swapped all their cards. Afterward, reinforce positive behavior: "I heard a lot of thought-provoking questions and in-depth answers."

6. **As time allows,** ask volunteers to share one highlight from their discussions. Encourage students to keep their cards for further reflection, or collect them all in one place as a classroom resource.

Quiz Trade in Action

An art teacher uses Quiz Trade to help students recall strategies they've learned to prepare for an upcoming project. She gives clear directions to set students up for success.

First she states the learning goal: "To prepare for our landscape project, you're going to collaborate with different partners to review strategies artists use to create a sense of dimension in 2-D works."

Then she explains students' roles and the timing: "Take out the three questions and answers related to creating dimension that you did for homework last night. On my signal, find a partner and take turns quizzing and responding to each other's questions."

She takes a few student questions, and then signals them to begin. After students share ideas with three different partners, the teacher asks volunteers to share with the class one strategy they'd like to try. She then connects these strategies to the upcoming landscape project.

Learning Goal Examples

English Language Arts	Math	Science	Social Studies
Front: "How is the house used as a plot device in 'The Landlady?'"	**Front:** "What is one fact about prime numbers?"	**Front:** "What is one way you can reduce air pollution?"	**Front:** "What roles did women take on during the Revolutionary War?"
Back: "Dahl builds suspense by slowly adding intriguing details as the story goes on."	**Back:** "The number 2 is the only prime number that is even."	**Back:** "By walking or riding a bike instead of driving a car."	**Back:** "Some women served as nurses, soldiers in disguise, and spies."

Pairs

Swap Meet

1. **Name the learning goal.** For example: "Let's see how many different solutions you can come up with to solve this math problem."

2. **Ask an open-ended question:** "Geneva earned $85 babysitting and is using it to buy school clothes. Prices are as follows: dresses $17.50, pants $11.50, shirts $7.50. How many different clothing combinations can Geneva buy?"

3. **Students work independently** to answer the question (or gather information as needed) and write their ideas down on their Swap Meet worksheet (see p. 65).

4. **After a few minutes,** signal for students to find a partner and swap an idea they came up with. A possible solution might be: four shirts, three pairs of pants, and one dress, giving Geneva 13 clothing options with $3 left over. Students can add any new ideas they hear to their worksheet. Allow 3–5 minutes for this exchange of ideas.

5. **Signal for students to find a new partner** and discuss the same question. Or, give them a different problem or question for this new round.

6. **Gather students back together.** As time allows, invite volunteers to share one solution to the problem. Then reinforce key positive behavior: "I heard many people listening carefully and waiting until the speaker finished before talking."

In Brief

Students answer a question or gather information (such as examples or evidence) about a topic and then exchange ideas with different partners.

*

Skills Practiced

Brainstorming

Reasoning

Staying focused

Summarizing

*

Time Frame

10–15 minutes

*

Materials

Paper or Swap Meet worksheet (p. 65)

Pencils

Timer

Learning Goal Examples

English Language Arts

"In the book *The One and Only Ivan* by Katherine Applegate, Ivan watches videos of other silverback gorillas before he's integrated into their habitat. What are some other ways zoos might help integrate animals that grew up in isolation?"

Related Arts (art)

"What's your plan for making a silhouette portrait?"

Swap Meet in Action

A world language teacher uses Swap Meet to have students recall what they've learned in the previous quarter and to practice conjugating verbs. To set students up for success, he takes a minute to provide clear directions.

"You're going to reflect on and share with partners the many things we've done and all you've accomplished this quarter," he says. "This will also be an opportunity for you to practice and reinforce your skills with conjugating verbs."

Then he explains everyone's roles and the timing: "Using the appropriate verb tense, each of you will write one or two statements that describe an activity we've done or something you've learned in class. You'll have three minutes to write your statements. Then, when I ring the chime, everyone will stand and find a partner to share with. After you've swapped statements, you'll find a new partner and repeat the process. When you've added three new statements to your list, return to your tables. Any questions?"

At the end of the activity, the teacher collects everyone's papers and creates an anchor chart for the class to use as they move into the next quarter.

Learning Goal Examples

Science

"How might you prepare for a volcanic eruption? A hurricane? Another natural disaster?"

Social Studies

"Find evidence in this essay that supports or counters this statement by Susan B. Anthony: 'The older I get, the greater power I seem to have to help the world; I am like a snowball—the further I am rolled the more I gain.'"

Pairs

In Brief

Students practice comparing and contrasting two topics as a way to visually and verbally articulate similarities and differences between two ideas.

*

Skills Practiced

Agreeing and disagreeing respectfully

Brainstorming

Summarizing

Synthesizing

*

Time Frame

10–15 minutes

*

Materials

Large paper or Venn diagram template (p. 66)

Timer

*

Variation

Students work in groups of four: two are presenters and two are reporters.

Venn-ting

HOW TO DO IT

1. **Name the learning goal.** For example: "You'll be exploring the similarities and differences between tropical and temperate forests."

2. **Pair students and assign roles:** reporter, presenter (see p. 5). Remind students about the importance of cooperation: "Name some ways both partners' ideas will be included."

3. **Have each pair set up and label** a Venn diagram (see p. 66), using the two topics you named.

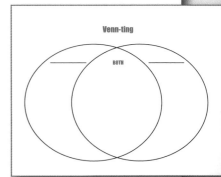

4. **Give students 3–5 minutes** to brainstorm ideas (with a 30-second warning before time's up). State the number of similarities and differences students should try to identify.

5. **The reporter from each pair** roams the room looking at other diagrams. The presenter stays put and explains their work to the other reporters. Allow reporters to visit two or three different diagrams and stay for 1–2 minutes at each.

6. **Reporters return to their original partners** and discuss what they learned. Give students a few minutes to add to or revise their original diagrams. Reinforce positive behavior: "I noticed a back-and-forth of ideas taking place. That's a good way for everyone to deepen their learning."

―――――――――― **Learning Goal Examples** ――――――――――

English Language Arts

The plots of *The Giver* by Lois Lowry and *Wonder* by R. J. Palacio

Math

Geometry and algebra

Venn-ting in Action

A 7th grade science class is completing a unit on skeletal-muscular systems. The teacher pairs students up and assigns each student one side of a Venn diagram. One side is labeled "frog" and the other is labeled "human." She gives clear directions to set students up for success.

First she states the learning goal: "You're going to compare and contrast two skeletal-muscular systems by creating Venn diagrams with a partner."

She points to a blank Venn diagram: "Label your side of the Venn diagram with your assigned skeletal-muscular system. You'll have five minutes to list 4–6 facts about it, using your notes and textbook. I'll give a 30-second warning and then, when time's up, you'll have three more minutes to work together to identify 4–6 similarities between the two systems. List these in the diagram's center."

After checking to see if anyone has questions, she releases students to work. When time's up, reporters visit other tables and presenters explain their work. After everyone updates their diagrams, they post them to review and discuss as a whole group. The teacher uses this time to correct any lingering misunderstandings.

Learning Goal Examples

Science	Social Studies	Technology
Photosynthesis and cellular respiration	The American Revolution and the French Revolution	Computers and the human brain

Pairs

Walk and Talk

In Brief

Students walk with partners and discuss a given topic or question as a way to re-energize and spark deeper thinking.

*

Skills Practiced

Exchanging ideas

Reasoning

Staying on topic

Summarizing

Voicing an opinion

*

Time Frame

3–8 minutes

*

Materials

Timer

*

Variation

Students audio-record their conversations as they walk, using a smartphone or other recording device, for use as notes or as a short presentation.

HOW TO DO IT

1. **Name the learning goal.** For example: "Time to renew your mental energy. I'm going to pose a question from what we learned about the Civil Rights Movement, and you're going to walk around the room with a partner to discuss it."

2. **Pair students with someone they don't normally work with** (or have them choose on their own). Remind students about strategies for sharing ideas: "What might help you dig deeper into this topic when doing the Walk and Talk?"

3. **Pose a topic or question:** "In what ways did musicians, such as John Coltrane and Pete Seeger, contribute to the Civil Rights Movement?" Remind students of the expectations for safe movement and voice volume.

4. **Allow 2–3 minutes for the Walk and Talk.** Provide a 30-second warning signal (or set a timer) for the whole class to regather. For example: You might have students walk up and down a hallway, or do two laps around the gym, as you observe.

5. **Invite each pair (or a few volunteers) to report one idea** discussed or to summarize their discussion for the whole class. Reinforce positive behavior: "Wow! I heard a lot of animated conversation about the importance of music to the Civil Rights Movement."

Learning Goal Examples

English Language Arts

"In the book *Sounder* by William H. Armstrong, how might the boy's life have been different if his father had not been arrested? Recall details from the book to back up your reasoning."

Math

"How are positive and negative numbers used together to describe quantities such as temperatures or elevations?"

Walk and Talk in Action

During a track and field unit, a PE teacher uses Walk and Talk as a warm-up activity to have students recall and share strategies for passing the baton in a relay race.

After everyone has gathered together, she states the learning goal: "To prepare you for running relays, you're going to do a Walk and Talk. This will get your body moving and give you a chance to talk about strategies for passing and receiving the baton before we actually run some relays."

Because students have done Walk and Talk before, she briefly reviews the expectations and timing: "First lap, just partner A talks. Second lap, partner B responds and offers additional tips and ideas. Play rock-paper-scissors to decide who's A and who's B. Two laps of brisk walking should take you about four minutes. When you finish or hear my whistle, return to the center circle for today's huddle."

After asking if anyone has questions, she pauses for five seconds. Since there are no questions, she signals students to start walking.

When students meet back in the center circle, the teacher invites them to share their strategies for passing and receiving the baton, and then they practice them in relay teams.

Learning Goal Examples

Science
"Recalling evidence from our insect unit, do you think ambush bugs make good pets? Why or why not?"

Technology
"Who are you interviewing for your video-blog project, and what questions are you planning to ask?"

In Brief

Pairs of students
(or small groups or the
whole class) "splash"
words or phrases onto
paper and explore
how they connect to
a topic or question.

*

Skills Practiced

Creative thinking

Making inferences

Public speaking

Summarizing

Synthesizing

*

Time Frame

10–12 minutes

*

Materials

Paper or Word Splash
template (p. 67)

Pen or pencil

*

Variation

For previewing, display
a premade word splash
about a topic the class
will be studying and
have students add
to it as they learn.

Word Splash

HOW TO DO IT

1. **Name the learning goal.** For example: "With a partner, you're going to brainstorm words related to our unit on the Middle East and then splash these words onto your paper."

2. **Pair students and assign roles:** recorder, presenter (see p. 5).

3. **Allow 2–3 minutes for brainstorming** and another 3–5 minutes for recorders to create the word splash using blank paper or the Word Splash template (see p. 67). Encourage students to think creatively: "How might you stretch your thinking to find words that relate to the Middle East and go beyond the unit vocabulary words?"

4. **Signal for pairs to finish** their word splashes (give a 15- to 30-second warning). Then have each presenter or a few volunteers display and briefly explain to the whole class how their word splash relates to the topic. Encourage recorders to add any new words they hear to their splashes. To extend the activity, have students define key terms and/or use them in sentences.

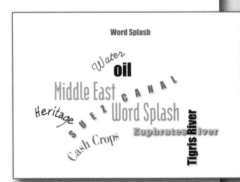

5. **Reinforce positive behavior:** "You put a lot of effort into brainstorming words that have a strong connection to the Middle East. This will help you better understand this region whenever you need to talk or write about it."

6. **Have students post their word splashes** on the class bulletin board for future reference and to use as a study guide.

Word Splash in Action

A drama teacher assigns small groups different characters from the play they're studying. He uses Word Splash to help them build a deeper understanding of each character and of the play overall.

Even though students have done Word Splash before, he gives them directions to make sure everyone is clear on the expectations: "In your groups, you're going to create a word splash that reflects the character I assigned you. Take three minutes to brainstorm and another three minutes to splash ideas onto your chart paper. I'll signal when there are 30 seconds left for brainstorming and for splashing words. Remember to choose a recorder and a presenter—and that everyone is expected to contribute ideas. To wrap things up, each group will have a minute or so to present their word splash to the whole class."

The teacher asks if anyone has questions, responds to a few, and then starts the timer. After the presentations, he displays the word splashes and encourages students to use them as references and add to them as they continue their study of the play.

Learning Goal Examples

English Language Arts	Math	Related Arts	Science
Short story; essay; novel the class has read/is reading	Pre-algebra; probability; number theory	Music genres; painting styles; library resources	Soil, water, and farming; energy resources; climate change

Amazing Analogies

In Brief

In small groups (or pairs), students explore analogies that relate a topic they're learning to a common object or activity as a way to deepen their understanding of that topic.

*

Skills Practiced

Brainstorming

Creative thinking

Giving meaningful feedback

Synthesizing

*

Time Frame

8–12 minutes

*

Materials

Timer

*

Variation

Groups come up with the topics and/or common objects or practices themselves.

H O W   T O   D O   I T

1. **Name the learning goal.** For example: "You're going to fully examine the characters in *To Kill a Mockingbird* through analogies."

2. **Assign roles:** recorder, presenter (see p. 5).

3. **Identify a content-related topic** and ask how it's related to something else such as a common object or activity: "How is Atticus Finch like a calendar?" Remind students how to work well together in groups: "What will you do if you disagree with someone's idea?"

4. **Set the timer.** Groups take 1–2 minutes to come up with reasons and evidence to support the analogy. A student might say: "Atticus Finch is like a calendar because you can always count on him, any day of the week." Recorders write down their group's ideas. Give a 15- to 30-second warning before time is up.

5. **When time is up, each group's presenter shares one** of the group's ideas with the whole class. Reinforce positive behavior: "You asked your classmates thoughtful questions to clarify your understanding."

6. **Repeat for 3–5 more content topics and common objects.**

———————— Learning Goal Examples ————————

English Language Arts

"How are the book genres we've been studying like school hallways?"

Math

"How are rational numbers like a lunch tray?"

Amazing Analogies in Action

A 7th grade social studies class finished their small group presentations on various forms of government. To deepen students' understanding after these presentations, the teacher uses Amazing Analogies. She gives clear directions to set students up for success.

First she names the learning goal: "You're going to wrap up this unit on government by brainstorming analogies that compare different types of government to items around the school."

Then she explains everyone's roles and the timing: "Each group needs a recorder and a presenter. Everyone in the group is expected to contribute ideas. For each round, I'll state an analogy and you'll have three minutes to brainstorm your responses with your group. I'll give a 15-second warning before time is up. When you hear my signal, look over the recorder's list and decide on one idea that your presenter will share with the whole group."

The teacher answers questions and then starts the activity: "First analogy: How is a democracy like a bowl of soup?" After students share their reasons and evidence to explain the analogy, she challenges them with a few more analogies on various forms of government. Afterward, she feels confident of their grasp of this content.

Learning Goal Examples

Related Arts (music)

"How is a half note like a calculator?"

Science

"How is the water cycle like a basketball?"

Social Studies

"How is the process of amending the U.S. Constitution like cooking?"

Around-the-Clock

In Brief

Going clockwise, each student poses a question and the other group members take turns responding.

✳

Skills Practiced

Asking and answering questions thoughtfully

Distinguishing fact from opinion

Reasoning

Strategizing

✳

Time Frame

3–10 minutes

✳

Materials

Clock Partners placemats (p. 56)

Timer

✳

Variation

Each student takes a turn sharing something they're looking forward to learning, and teammates take turns asking them to elaborate.

HOW TO DO IT

1. **Name the learning goal.** For example: "As a way to wrap up this unit, let's analyze what you've learned from the article on the Great Lakes."

2. **Put a Clock Partners placemat** (see p. 56) in the center of each group. Students use the placemat to determine whether they are the 12 o'clock, 3 o'clock, 6 o'clock, or 9 o'clock person. (If needed, model how to take turns clockwise.)

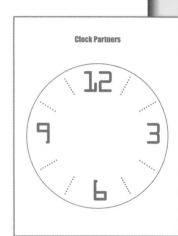

Clock Partners

3. **Give students a topic for discussion** and have the 12 o'clock teammate ask the first question (generated either by the teacher or by students). A student might ask: "According to this article, how have humans impacted the Great Lakes?"

4. **Teammates answer clockwise:**

   3 o'clock • "Page two describes how industrial pollution has harmed fish life."

   6 o'clock • "Here on page four, it talks about how increasing demand for public water supplies pose future threats to the lakes."

   9 o'clock • "The very first paragraph notes how the lakes are still important for shipping and ships are safer than ever, but spills keep happening."

5. **The 3 o'clock person asks another question about the topic.** Teammates again answer clockwise.

6. **Repeat until every person has asked a question.** Reinforce positive behavior: "Your questions were clear and specific. And I heard many people respond in a respectful tone of voice."

Around-the-Clock in Action

The 8th grade chorus is practicing an a capella piece for their winter concert. Students need to know their own parts and how all four parts will work together. The teacher adapts Around-the-Clock so each group has a student representing each part. He gives clear directions to set students up for a successful practice.

First he names the learning goal: "Before you practice singing as a whole group, you're going to do Around-the-Clock to help you first hear the individual parts and then hear what all four parts sound like together in a smaller group setting."

Then he explains student roles and the timing: "When I give the signal, each member of your group will take turns singing their part of the first two phrases—going clockwise starting with 12 o'clock. After everyone has sung their part individually, your group will sing the parts together."

The teacher asks if anyone has questions and then signals students to begin. This structure enables the students to hone their individual parts and hear what all four parts sound like together—in a smaller setting—before trying to sing as a whole group.

Learning Goal Examples

English Language Arts

Exploring informational texts

Math

Reviewing formulas before a test

Related Arts (art)

Summarizing techniques and elements of different artistic movements

Science

Recalling an invention recently studied

Social Studies

Previewing or reviewing a chapter or chapter section

Small Groups

Beat the Clock

In Brief

Students do timed challenges to recall information about a topic they're learning as a way to strengthen their understanding of that content.

*

Skills Practiced

Brainstorming

Strategizing

Summarizing

Synthesizing

*

Time Frame

5–10 minutes

*

Materials

Large paper

Pencils

Timer

*

Variation

Groups come up with their own Beat the Clock challenges.

1. **Name the learning goal.** For example: "You'll do timed challenges to boost your memory of math facts."

2. **Group (or pair) students and assign roles:** recorder, presenter (see p. 5).

3. **Identify 4–6 content-related challenges in advance.** Decide how much time to allow students for each challenge (60 seconds or less is optimal to keep the activity moving). Start with easier challenges. Increase the difficulty with each round:

   Numbers between 100 and 200 divisible by 4 (30 seconds)

   then

   Numbers between 100 and 200 divisible by 8.5 (60 seconds)

4. **Name the first challenge and set the timer.** Teammates come up with as many answers as possible before time is up while the recorder writes them down (give a 5-second warning). Provide reminders as needed: "What's a strategy you can use to keep ideas flowing when you have limited time for brainstorming?"

5. **When time is up, presenters share one of their group's ideas** with the class.

6. **Repeat for remaining challenges.** Remember to reinforce positive behavior: "I noticed small groups [or pairs] collaborating well, with multiple people sharing."

Learning Goal Examples

Health–Nutrition

Types of nutrients essential to human health (30 seconds)

Sources of protein (60 seconds)

Related Arts (art)

Famous painters (20 seconds)

Examples of painting styles from the 21st century (45 seconds)

Beat the Clock in Action

As the 6th graders wrap up a unit on poetry, the teacher uses Beat the Clock to help them solidify their understanding of figurative language. First he names the learning goal: "You're going to do Beat the Clock to show that you know types of figurative language and can recognize them in a poem."

Then he assigns students to pairs and assigns roles. Next he explains the action and timing: "I'm going to give you two challenges to work on with your partner. You'll take turns being the recorder, and it's fine for the recorder to contribute ideas as well as writing down their partner's ideas. For the first challenge, you'll have 20 seconds to name four types of figurative language from among those we've been studying, and I'll give a 5-second warning."

He invites questions and then continues: "For the second challenge, you'll look for and label examples of figurative language in a poem I'll hand out. The other partner will be the recorder, and you'll have 60 seconds to find as many examples as you can. I'll give a 10-second warning."

The teacher answers a couple more questions and starts the activity. After each challenge, he invites presenters to share their group's work and offers corrections as needed.

Learning Goal Examples

Science

Parts of an atom (10 seconds)

Elements in the periodic table (45 seconds)

Social Studies

U.S. states (30 seconds)

U.S. capitals (60 seconds)

Consensus Mapping

In Brief

Students identify the main ideas of a given topic by reaching group consensus.

*

Skills Practiced

Agreeing and disagreeing respectfully

Persuading others

Reasoning

Strategizing

*

Time Frame

8–12 minutes

*

Materials

Chart paper or Consensus Map template (p. 57)

Pencils

Timer

*

Variation

Use this activity to build community by reaching consensus on non-academic topics (top five movies of the year, books every student should read).

HOW TO DO IT

1. **Name the learning goal.** For example: "You're going to explore scientific breakthroughs in more depth."

2. **Each group creates** their Consensus Map and each student chooses a quadrant (see example shown here and on p. 57).

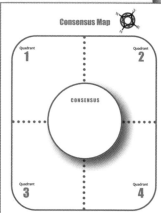

3. **Name a specific topic,** such as top scientific breakthroughs of the early 20th century. Students have two minutes to list their ideas in their own quadrant. Set a target number of responses. Signal a 15-second warning before time is up.

4. **Going clockwise, students take turns** reading their list to their group. (Listeners may add new ideas to their quadrant.) Then each student circles three ideas in their quadrant to nominate for consensus. For example, a student might choose powered flight (Wilbur and Orville Wright), two new radioactive elements (Marie Curie), and penicillin (Andrew Fleming).

5. **Students take turns nominating their circled ideas** for consensus (one idea per turn) and state a brief reason for their choice. If all members agree, the student records this idea in the consensus circle.

6. **The activity ends when the group** reaches a predetermined number of items in their consensus circle (such as "top three scientific breakthroughs") or after a set amount of time has elapsed.

7. **To extend the activity,** record each group's consensus items and as a whole class try to reach a common consensus. Reinforce positive behavior: "I saw a lot of compromise as your team worked to agree on which ideas to include."

Consensus Mapping in Action

Student council members conducted a survey to gauge school spirit. After analyzing the results, a school counselor uses Consensus Mapping to help the council members decide on next steps for improving school spirit. She assigns groups in advance and gives clear directions to set students up for successful decision-making.

First she names the learning goal: "You're going to split into groups of four and make consensus maps to find ways to improve school spirit."

Then she explains each council member's role and the activity's timing and transitions: "In their quadrant, each member of the group will write their own ideas for improving school spirit on the basis of the survey results. You'll have two minutes to list your ideas. I'll give you a 15-second warning to wrap up. When time's up, take turns sharing your list with your group and circle common ideas. Then, as a group, come to agreement on one idea to be the 'next step' for improving school spirit."

The school counselor asks if anyone has questions and then sets the timer: "Split into your groups and begin." Afterward, each group shares out their consensus idea and students vote on which one the student council will focus on first.

Learning Goal Examples

English Language Arts	Health/PE	Math	Social Studies
Stories/books read in class that best represent empathy	Top sports that promote teamwork	Top calculating tools for engineers	Five customs that are common among many world cultures

Four Corners

HOW TO DO IT

1. **Name the learning goal.** For example, as part of a discussion about *Dragonwings* by Laurence Yep: "You're going to dig deeper into the book's main characters to explore different aspects of each character."

2. **Pose a question that has four possible responses:** "In the early chapters of the book, what in your opinion is the greatest challenge Moon Shadow faces, and why?"

3. **Designate one corner of the room for each response:**

    Corner one—His physical journey to the United States

    Corner two—Leaving his mother and grandmother

    Corner three—Being a new immigrant in the United States

    Corner four—Discovering there is no Golden Mountain

4. **Give students a minute to reflect on their choice.** When time is up, they move to the corresponding corner. Reinforce positive behavior: "I noticed you carefully considered your choice before moving to that corner."

5. **In their corners, students discuss in small groups (or pairs)** why they made their choice and provide reasons and evidence to support their decision.

6. **Allow about 30 seconds for each person to share** or 1–2 minutes in total for a more free-flowing discussion. Provide a 10-second warning before time is up.

7. **Repeat,** with a new question and responses, as time allows.

In Brief

Students choose a response to a teacher-posed question that best reflects their thinking or interests. They move to the corner representing that response and discuss it in small groups (or pairs).

✳

Skills Practiced

Agreeing and disagreeing respectfully

Reasoning

Voicing an opinion

✳

Time Frame

5–10 minutes
(3 or 4 rounds)

✳

Materials

Timer

Four Corners in Action

After students explore various types of poems, the English language arts teacher uses Four Corners so they can share their perspectives on them. She labels the corners "prose," "haiku," "rhyming couplet," and "limerick" and then directs students on how to choose corners and discuss their choice successfully.

First she names the learning goal: "You're going to use Four Corners to share your perspectives on the types of poetry we've been studying."

Then she explains roles, timing, and transitions: "This activity should move quickly. For each round, I'll make a statement to guide your reflection on poetry. You'll move to the corner that best represents your perspective. Then you'll pair up with someone and take 30 seconds each to share about your choice. I'll give a 10-second warning for you to wrap up your sharing. Then we'll repeat this with another statement for two more rounds."

She answers questions and then begins the activity: "Round one: Move to the corner that represents a type of poetry you most like to read." This activity helps the teacher gauge student interest and better meet their needs as they study each type of poetry in more depth.

Learning Goal Examples

Math

"Based on the last three survey results, who do you think will win the election, and why?"

Responses: candidate A, B, C, D

Related Arts (art)

"Which of the following qualities do you find most powerful in this painting?"

Responses: use of space/composition, line/shape, texture/brushwork, color

Science

"What does this organ do, and why is it essential for good health?"

Responses: heart, lungs, kidneys, liver

Social Studies

"Which aspect of industrialization do you think changed U.S. cities the most, and why?"

Responses: population growth, labor unrest, technological innovations, expanding democracy

Jigsaws

In Brief

To explore content in greater depth, students work in small groups to become "experts" on one aspect of a topic and then share that knowledge in a "jigsaw" group.

*

Skills Practiced

Exchanging ideas

Staying on topic

Summarizing

Synthesizing

*

Time Frame

15–30 minutes (depending on the content being analyzed)

*

Materials

Copies of articles, photos, or other content

Paper or Jigsaws worksheet (p. 60)

Pencils

HOW TO DO IT

1. **Name the learning goal.** For example: "I have three short articles that give interesting perspectives on rock formations. You'll each read one article and then discuss it twice—first with those who have read the same article, and then with those who haven't."

2. **Divide students evenly into "expert" groups.** Name one facilitator per group (see p. 5) and assign each group a short article (or section of content): groups A and B read and discuss an article on sedimentary rock, groups C and D igneous rocks, and groups E and F metamorphic rocks. (For longer texts, assign reading ahead of time.) Offer a quick reminder about expectations: "Remember to listen respectfully to each other's ideas."

3. **Give groups five minutes to read their article** and another five minutes to agree on its key ideas and write them down on their Jigsaws worksheet (see p. 60).

4. **Members of each expert group count off.** All ones form a "jigsaw" group, twos another, and so on. Every jigsaw group will have experts on each article.

5. **In their jigsaw groups, students share the key ideas of their article** and write new information down on their worksheets. Give reminders as needed: "How will you make sure there's time for questions and comments in your group?"

6. **As a whole class, summarize the key ideas of each article** to ensure that everyone has the same understanding of the content.

Learning Goal Examples

English Language Arts	**Math**	**Related Arts (music)**
Short stories by 20th century writers	Articles about the use of math in different professions	Audio recordings by different composers

Jigsaws in Action

A drama teacher regularly uses Jigsaws to have students explore and share ideas about the plays they're studying. She gives clear directions to help students successfully learn key developments.

First she states their task: "You're going to read the first act of the play today. You'll each read one scene and then discuss it twice: first in an expert group where everyone reads the same scene and then in a jigsaw group with those who have read the other scenes."

After assigning students their scenes and their expert and jigsaw groups, she explains roles, timing, and transitions: "In your expert group, focus on the important developments for the characters and the plot. Before we start reading and discussing, let's name some strategies we can use to make sure everyone has a chance to comment."

After taking a few questions, the teacher tells students they'll have 12 minutes to read and discuss their scenes, with a 30-second warning when it's time to wrap up. Next she sets the timer: "OK, begin!" Then, after the jigsaw discussions, she leads a whole class discussion to solidify students' understanding of the key developments of the play's first act.

Learning Goal Examples

Science

Video clips of different planets or ecosystems

Social Studies

A textbook chapter divided into sections

The Last Word

In Brief

Students work together to recall information through word association about a topic they've studied.

*

Skills Practiced

Brainstorming

Creative thinking

Public speaking

Summarizing

Synthesizing

*

Time Frame

5–10 minutes

*

Materials

Chart paper or interactive whiteboard

Markers

Timer

*

Variations

Each group comes up with their own key word for the topic.

Do this activity as a whole class.

HOW TO DO IT

1. **Name the learning goal.** For example: "Your goal is to brainstorm key terms and phrases related to our geometry and measurement unit." Remind students how to work efficiently: "What strategies and resources will help you in brainstorming?"

2. **Have students form small groups** and assign roles: recorder, presenter (see p. 5). Write the topic's key word, "geometry," vertically on the board or chart paper.

3. **Explain what students will do:** "Next to each letter in the word 'geometry,' you'll write a word or phrase that starts with that letter and has something to do with geometry. Be sure you know what each word or phrase means. If you get stuck, it's OK to leave a letter blank. You'll have 4 minutes, and I'll give you a 30-second warning before time is up."

4. **Set the timer and start the activity:** "OK, begin."

5. **Groups write and define their words or phrases** and discuss how these relate to the topic. Recorders list their group's ideas:
    Geometric figure
    Edge
    Obtuse angle
    Measure
    Equilateral
    Trapezoid
    Ray
    Y-axis

6. **Ask presenters to share one of their group's words** and its relation to the topic. After each group has shared, open up the discussion to include any related words or phrases that weren't listed.

The Last Word in Action

An 8th grade English language arts teacher uses The Last Word for students to review different types of essays that they've studied and practiced writing in her class: expository, persuasive, and narrative. She sets students up for success by giving them clear directions.

"You're going to work in groups to review the key elements of the type of essay I assign you. For example: If your group has 'persuasive,' think of words and phrases that relate to persuasive essays that start with the letter 'p,' such as 'powerful,' then 'e,' and so on. Then create a Last Word poster to use as a reference guide."

Then she explains roles and the activity's time frame: "Each group needs a recorder and presenter, and everyone is expected to brainstorm. You'll have four minutes for brainstorming, and four more minutes to create your Last Word poster. I'll ring the chime to let you know when it's time to start wrapping up each of these tasks. Presenters will then share one of their group's words."

She asks if anyone has questions, has students assemble into their groups, and gives the signal to begin: "Start brainstorming."

As presenters share words from their Last Word posters, the teacher notices that students have gained a better understanding of each essay type. Afterward, students display their Last Word posters as anchor charts on a classroom bulletin board.

Learning Goal Examples

English Language Arts	Science	Social Studies	Technology
Expository	Biotic factors	Social institutions	Transforming the world
Subject	Ice-cap	Oppression	Electricity dependent
Summary	Oceans	Culture	Communication
Analyzing evidence	Mountains	Immigrant	Hardware
Your analysis	Ecosystem	Ethnic groups	Netiquette
	Savanna	Traditional economy	Online resources
		Youth	Links
			Operating system
			Global connections
			Y [blank]

Small Groups

Maître d'

In Brief

Students form "tables" of 2–4 to exchange a wide range of ideas.

*

Skills Practiced

Reasoning

Staying focused

Voicing an opinion

*

Time Frame

7–10 minutes

*

Materials

None

*

Variation

Use this activity to build community by discussing favorites, such as books, movies, or hobbies.

1. **Name the learning goal.** For example: "You're going to form different table sizes [standing groups] to share ideas about our unit on healthy living."

2. **Remind students about the expectations** for forming new table groups, emphasizing the importance of being inclusive, friendly, and respectful: "What will you do to make sure everyone is included?" (If needed, model how to move about the room safely.)

3. **Call out a grouping, starting with "Table for two."** Students quickly form pairs of their own choosing (with one table of three, if needed).

4. **Ask a question to focus the discussion:** "How might you increase your weekly physical activity?" Give students 1–2 minutes to share (with a 15-second warning). Reinforce positive behavior: "I heard a lot of encouraging words when people got stuck on an idea to share."

5. **Call out "Table for three," have students form new groups,** and ask the same question or a new one. After groups have discussed this question, call out "Table for four." Repeat as time allows, continuing to vary the table numbers.

6. **To extend the learning,** bring everyone back together and ask a few volunteers to share highlights from one of their conversations.

Learning Goal Examples

English Language Arts

"How are the book and movie versions of Rick Riordan's *The Lightning Thief* different? Alike? Which did you like better, and why?"

Math

"What are some ways you use fractions in real life? How are fractions and decimals alike? Which is easier to use, and why?"

Maître d' in Action

A 6th grade art teacher models various strategies for applying different glazes to a piece of pottery and shows the results of each method after firing in a kiln. He uses Maître d' to give students opportunities to discuss what they noticed in his demonstrations. Before students begin, the teacher gives clear directions to set them up for success.

First he names the learning goal and explains roles and responsibilities: "You're going to form different standing groups to discuss what you noticed about each glazing method. Everyone is expected to share ideas and listen to everyone else's ideas. Remember our rule 'Be respectful, kind, and inclusive' when forming new groups."

Because he's noticed that students often struggle with transitions, he makes a point to explain how these will work for this activity: "For each round, I'll pose a question about my demonstration. You'll have two minutes to discuss it with your group. I'll give a 30-second warning to wrap up your conversations. Then I'll call out another table number and you'll form new groups."

After responding to a few clarifying questions, the teacher starts the activity: "Table for two! … What did you notice about the brush-on method I used?"

After several rounds of "table" discussions, the teacher ends the activity. Students use the new understanding gained from their discussions in planning how to glaze their own pottery pieces.

Learning Goal Examples

Science

"In what ways might you conserve water at home? At school? What role can government play in protecting our water supplies?"

Social Studies

"How is a totalitarian society different from a democratic society? How are they alike? How important is a written constitution for protecting people's freedoms?"

One-Sentence/One-Word Summaries

In Brief

Students write one sentence about a topic they studied and then choose one word that sums up their learning.

＊

Skills Practiced

Public speaking

Reasoning

Summarizing

Synthesizing

＊

Time Frame

5–8 minutes

＊

Materials

Paper

Pencils

Timer

＊

Variation

Use this activity as a quick way to assess students' learning: At various stopping points in the unit, ask them for a one-sentence or one-word summary to get a sense of their understanding.

HOW TO DO IT

1. **Name the learning goal.** For example: "You're going to wrap up our unit on Ancient Egypt's social structures by writing a summary sentence. Then as a class we'll choose one word that captures that learning."

2. **Arrange students into small groups and assign roles:** recorder, presenter (see p. 5). This can also be done as a whole class activity.

3. **Each group takes 2–3 minutes to come up with one sentence** that summarizes their new knowledge, and recorders write the sentence. A group might come up with: "Ancient Egypt's social pyramid has pharaohs and gods at the top; nobles, tradespeople, and craftspeople in the middle; and farmers, servants, and enslaved people at the bottom."

4. **Signal when time is up** and call on presenters to share their group's summary sentence. Clarify any misconceptions and reinforce positive behavior: "Your summaries show sharp thinking; they really get to the core ideas of this topic."

5. **After each group shares,** guide the whole class to collaborate on choosing one word—for example, "pyramid"—that captures the essence of all the summary sentences. As time allows, ask an open-ended question to prompt student reflection: "What strategies did you use to reach agreement on your summary sentences?"

Learning Goal Examples

English Language Arts

Poetry: "Poets use imagery, word repetition, rhythm, and onomatopoeia." (poetic devices)

Health/PE

Healthy Habits: "A healthy diet, managing stress, and a good night's sleep help boost brain power." (balance)

One-Sentence/One-Word Summaries in Action

A music teacher uses an adaptation of One-Sentence/One-Word Summaries to have students reflect on a new piece of music. To set students up for success, he first names the goal: "You've been listening to and learning to play this new piece. Now you'll have the chance to communicate its mood by creating a short musical phrase of your own that expresses that mood."

Next he assigns groups and clarifies everyone's responsibilities: "With your groups, talk about the composition and the mood each of you feels the piece expresses. Come up with your own musical phrase—no more than four measures' worth—that expresses that same mood. Then you'll take turns playing it for the others in your group."

The teacher explains how the timing and transitions will work: "You'll have two minutes to plan and then another two minutes to practice and revise your phrase before you play it for your group. I'll signal 15 seconds before you need to change tasks. Any questions? ... OK, get into your groups and begin."

After every group member has shared their musical phrase, the teacher asks for a few volunteers to play theirs for the whole group. He uses these as a jumping-off point to discuss the elements of the composition that help create the mood.

Learning Goal Examples

Math

Geometry: "Squares, rectangles, and rhombuses have four edges and four corners, and their interior angles add up to 360 degrees." (quadrilaterals)

Science

Environmental Science: "Acid rain is made up of sulfuric and nitric acids and can damage buildings, people, animals, plants, soil, and water." (air pollution)

Small Groups

In Brief

Students analyze a text or video/audio clip by stopping at designated points (that you choose ahead of time) and sharing ideas or posing questions.

*

Skills Practiced

Asking and answering questions thoughtfully

Summarizing

Synthesizing

*

Time Frame

10–20 minutes (depending on length of text/clips)

*

Materials

Copies of text

Computers/tablets (to access video/audio clips)

Paper or Say Something worksheet (p. 62)

Pencils

*

Variation

Students work in pairs.

Say Something

HOW TO DO IT

1. **Name the learning goal.** For example: "You're going to analyze this article on climate change by pausing after each section to make a comment or ask a question, going in order around your groups." Emphasize that what students say does not have to relate to what other members of their group say; they also should not respond to anyone's questions or comments at this point.

2. **Arrange students into small groups** and assign roles: recorder, presenter (see p. 5). Then hand out Say Something worksheets (see p. 62). Announce the stopping points as recorders write them down on their group's worksheet. Remind students of expectations: "How can you communicate in your group so that other groups can concentrate?"

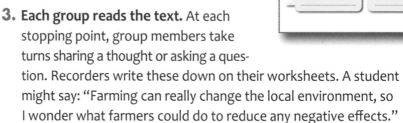

3. **Each group reads the text.** At each stopping point, group members take turns sharing a thought or asking a question. Recorders write these down on their worksheets. A student might say: "Farming can really change the local environment, so I wonder what farmers could do to reduce any negative effects."

4. **After finishing the entire text,** have presenters share out one of their group's comments or questions for the whole class. Reinforce positive behavior: "You paid attention to both the supporting details and the main ideas in this article."

5. **Read aloud any sections students found confusing** or that are worth emphasizing. To extend the activity, encourage students to respond to one another's questions and comments.

Say Something in Action

A PE teacher uses Say Something to help students focus on key elements of the different skills they'll practice in class that day. To set students up for success, she gives them clear directions.

First she names their task: "Today you're going to view some short video clips showcasing passing and dribbling strategies. Later you'll have an opportunity to practice these skills and strengthen your own passing and dribbling."

Next she explains how to do it: "After viewing each clip, you'll take turns sharing with your squad something specific that you noticed the players do. As each person shares, everyone else in your group will listen but not add to what was said. As a group, you'll have 60 seconds to Say Something after each clip. I'll blow the whistle when there are 10 seconds left on the clock."

Before showing the first clip, the teacher invites questions to make sure students understand their task. As students share in their groups, she observes and responds if students have questions. After viewing several clips and doing several rounds of Say Something, the students practice the skills while the teacher reinforces essential elements from the clips.

Learning Goal Examples

English Language Arts	**Math**	**Social Studies**	**Technology**
Video clip from a movie version of a book the class read	Chapter on building number sense	Essay on the Cold War	Audio clip from an interview with a public figure

Small Groups

Stay and Stray

In Brief

Students learn multiple ways to accomplish a task within a small group and then discover how other groups approached the same task.

*

Skills Practiced

Asking and answering questions thoughtfully

Giving meaningful feedback

Reasoning

Summarizing

Synthesizing

*

Time Frame

15–20 minutes

*

Materials

Paper or Stay and Stray worksheet (p. 64)

Pencils

Timer

1. **Name the learning goal.** For example: "Let's explore how many different ways you can solve this math problem."

2. **Group students and assign roles:** one presenter; other members are reporters (see p. 5). Hand out to each student blank paper or a Stay and Stray worksheet (see p. 64) and give the class a task to accomplish in their small groups: "Get to 1,000 by adding numbers that only include the digit 8." Presenters write their group's ideas on their worksheet.

   Stay and Stray

   | Group: | Group: | Group: |
   | Notes: | Notes: | Notes: |

3. **Allow 2–4 minutes for this group work.** Give a 30-second warning before time is up. Offer support as needed and reinforce positive behavior: "I'm hearing thoughtful suggestions for how to identify number patterns."

4. **Each group's reporters go to a new table.**

   • The presenter stays and shares their group's work for one minute with the reporters who come to their table.

   • Reporters take notes as the presenter shares.

   Repeat, with reporters traveling to two or more tables as time allows. Give reminders as needed: "Presenters, remember to allow time for questions at the end of your presentation."

5. **Reporters return to their groups and summarize** what they discovered about other groups' work. Presenters add these ideas to their worksheet. As time allows, groups can revise their original ideas. To extend the learning, ask reflective questions: "How did hearing other groups' ideas help you revise your own group's work?"

Stay and Stray in Action

In collaboration with the team's math and social studies teachers, 8th grade students are creating infographics in art class that persuade workers to open retirement accounts. The art teacher uses Stay and Stray throughout this project to facilitate students' giving and receiving feedback. To ensure everyone knows the expectations, the teacher gives clear directions each time they're about to do this activity.

She begins by reinforcing the learning goal: "You're going to learn about the progress everyone has made on their infographics project." Next she reminds students of their roles and responsibilities: "Each group has one presenter and two reporters. Reporters go to the other groups' tables and take notes while the presenter stays and talks about your group's progress."

To ensure smooth transitions, she also reviews the timing and transitions: "Presenters, you have one minute to describe your group's progress since our last class. Reporters, when I signal that time is up, move to another table. You'll get a chance to visit every group. Then return to your own group and summarize what you learned for your presenter. Any questions?" After pausing, and hearing no questions, she releases students to begin.

This structure gives students opportunities to present their work at each stage of the project (from initial ideas to final drafts), learn from other groups' ideas, and refine their work with their own groups.

Learning Goal Examples

Vocational/ Technology	English Language Arts	Science	Social Studies and Math
"Write the instructions for building a box out of wood."	"Write a haiku about school lunch."	"If you were the governor, what steps would you take to reduce urban pollution, and why?"	"Using your map app, choose a route an ambulance might take from our school to the hospital, and explain your choice."

World Café*

In Brief

Students move in and out of ongoing, small group conversations. This flowing, but still structured, format enables students to hear multiple perspectives on various topics or questions.

*

Skills Practiced

Agreeing and disagreeing respectfully

Reasoning

Staying focused

Voicing an opinion

*

Time Frame

10–15 minutes

*

Materials

None

HOW TO DO IT

1. **Name the learning goal.** For example: "You're going to move about the World Café, forming tables of four or five to discuss different technology devices."

2. **Assign each table a facilitator and give a discussion topic:** Table A, smartphone; Table B, tablet; Table C, video game console; and so on.

3. **Provide a question to focus the table discussions:** "What are some ways your device can be used to enhance your learning?" Remind students to stretch their thinking: "How can you expand your conversations to go beyond the ideas that first come up?"

4. **After 2–3 minutes, give a signal to wrap up conversations** and invite two or three students per table to change tables. Pose a new focus question or use the same one for new table groups to discuss. Reinforce positive behavior: "I'm hearing a lot of different ideas being shared. You're thinking much more globally about these topics than last week."

5. **Do several more rounds of table changes as time allows.** Then bring everyone back together and invite several volunteers to share out one idea from their table discussions.

Learning Goal Examples

English Language Arts

Table topics: similes, metaphors, idioms, hyperbole.

"How might you use your figurative language in a short story, and why?"

Math

Table topics: mean, median, mode, range.

"How would you define your term and use it in statistics?"

Science

Table topics: crust, mantle, outer core, inner core.

"What are some characteristics of your layer of Earth?"

Social Studies

Table topics: family, cultural, educational, political.

"What role does your social institution have in society?"

*An adaptation of the World Café™, a structured conversational process, found at www.theworldcafe.com.

World Café in Action

A choir director uses World Café to have students reflect on what went well and what was bumpy at their winter concert and to capture their ideas about what would make for a stronger spring concert. He gives clear directions to set students up for successful reflection.

First he names the learning goal: "You're going to have opportunities to reflect, share opinions, and hear others' perspectives on our first concert. Your conversations will offer some ideas for us to consider as we plan for our spring concert."

Then he explains roles, timing, and transitions: "On each table, you'll see a question related to the concert. You'll hold an open discussion while being mindful to make sure that all voices are heard. Some topics you can expect to discuss are: your overall performance, audience engagement, and song choice. For each round, you'll have about 3–4 minutes to chat with your table group. When I ring the chime, that will be your cue to wrap up and then two or three of you will move to a new table. Any questions?" After answering a few, he rings the chime.

Afterward, the teacher opens up the discussion to the whole class, asking volunteers to share ideas for the spring concert.

Fact or Fiction

In Brief

Students write true and false statements about a topic they're studying and the class tries to identify which statements are false.

*

Skills Practiced

Brainstorming

Creative thinking

Making inferences

Public speaking

Summarizing

*

Time Frame

5–8 minutes

*

Materials

Index cards or Fact or Fiction worksheet (p. 59)

Timer

*

Variation

Students can write true and false statements about themselves to get to know each other better. Discuss topics students might consider (hobbies, interests, favorites, etc.).

HOW TO DO IT

1. **Name the learning goal.** For example: "Your goal today is to discover interesting facts about the scientists you're studying."

2. **Explain that students will have 2–3 minutes** to write on an index card or their Fact or Fiction worksheet (see p. 59) two factual statements about the topic, plus one statement that isn't true but sounds like it could be. A student studying Isaac Newton might write:

   • Newton formulated the Law of Universal Gravity. (T)

   • Newton formulated the Three Laws of Motion. (T)

   • Newton discovered the first four moons of Jupiter. (F)

3. **Students take turns reading their statements** to the class (or just to a small group), and classmates try to identify which statement is false. Reinforce positive behavior: "I noticed careful listening before you said which statements you thought were false."

4. **Optional:** If done as a small group activity, conclude by inviting a few students to share with the whole class.

Learning Goal Examples

English Language Arts

A protagonist is the main character. (T)

The antagonist is the character that tries to stop the protagonist from reaching his or her goal. (T)

A secondary character is the second character mentioned in the story. (F)

Math

An addend is a number placed at the end of a sequence of numbers. (F)

A quotient is the answer to a division problem. (T)

The distance between two rational numbers on the number line is the absolute value of their difference. (T)

Fact or Fiction in Action

A 6th grade health class is beginning a "healthy habits for healthy living" unit. The teacher uses Fact or Fiction to get an initial sense of students' understanding of healthy eating, sleeping, and exercise.

"You're going to use Fact or Fiction," he says, "to see how much you already know about this topic before we start our unit on healthy habits for healthy living."

After reviewing some examples with students, he has them count off by threes and then assigns topics: eating (ones), sleeping (twos), and exercise (threes). "You'll have three minutes to write down two statements that you think are true about your topic and one statement that you think is false. I'll give a 30-second warning so you can finalize your statements. When time's up, you'll share your statements and we'll try to figure out which statement is false. Any questions? OK, go!"

As students work, the teacher notices that many of them struggle to write statements about nutrition and to determine which of their peers' statements about nutrition are false. He tactfully corrects misunderstandings and uses this information to adjust the scope and sequence of the unit so that students have more time for nutrition education.

Learning Goal Examples

Related Arts (drama)

"Blocking" refers to actors' movements on stage. (T)

"Aside" refers to one side of the stage. (F)

"Dress rehearsal" refers to performing in full costume before the play opens to the public. (T)

Social Studies

An immigrant is a person who comes to live in a foreign country permanently. (T)

A migrant worker is someone who works in the same place all year long. (F)

A naturalized citizen is a non-citizen of a country who becomes a citizen of that country. (T)

Whole Class

In Brief

Students share content knowledge and make connections to better understand what they are learning.

*

Skills Practiced

Brainstorming

Creative thinking

Making inferences

Public speaking

*

Time Frame

5–7 minutes
(you can read a few cards/worksheets each period over the course of multiple classes)

*

Materials

Index cards or Shared Truths worksheet (p. 63)

Pencils

*

Variation

Use this structure to help students (as a whole class or in small groups) share about themselves so they get to know each other better.

Shared Truths

HOW TO DO IT

1. **Name the learning goal.** For example: "You'll be reviewing the similarities and differences among periodic elements."

2. **Assign each student a relevant topic,** such as one periodic element. Tell them not to share it with anyone at this point. Pass out index cards or Shared Truths worksheets (see p. 63). Give students a few minutes to write three facts about their element, using their notes or other resources (or assign this in advance). For example:

   • Something that would also be true for **most** other students' elements: has more than two protons.

   • Something that would only be true for **some** students' elements: is flammable.

   • Something that would be true for **just a few or no other** students' elements: humans breathe in while plants "breathe out" this element (oxygen).

3. **Collect the cards or worksheets.** Randomly choose one and read the statements.

   • If the first statement is true for their element, students stand up.

   • If the second statement is also true for their element, they remain standing while other students sit down.

   • After the third statement is read, whoever is still standing reveals their element.

4. **Reinforce students' efforts:** "Everyone worked hard to identify new connections during this activity."

5. **Over the next few days,** go through 2–3 cards or worksheets until all have been read.

Shared Truths in Action

Throughout the year, a 7th grade team of teachers uses Shared Truths during Advisory to strengthen students' peer-to-peer affiliation. By sharing facts about themselves, students discover many things in common with their peers.

Here's how one teacher sets students up for successful sharing. First she names the learning goal and the expectations: "You're going to use Shared Truths to see how much you have in common and to learn a few new things about each other. On your worksheet, write down a statement that is true for you and might also be true for many others in our group, a statement that may be true for some of you, and a statement that is most likely only true about you."

Then she explains the timing: "You'll have five minutes. I'll give a 30-second warning so you can finalize your statements. When time's up, hand your worksheet to me. I'll read two or three out loud each day over the next few days. When I read a statement, if it's true for you, stand up. Stay standing until you hear a statement that isn't true for you and then sit. Pay attention to who is standing for each statement." After answering students' questions, she starts the timer.

This teacher uses what she's learned about students from Shared Truths to help her form small groups more purposefully in her math class. Another team teacher notices how previously unconnected students from his Advisory group are now working much more collaboratively in his social studies class.

Learning Goal Examples

English Language Arts
Different types of poems

Most: "I have rhythm to my words."

Some: "I have a set number of stanzas or lines."

Few or no other: "My line pattern is five syllables, seven syllables, five syllables." (haiku)

Math
Two-dimensional figures

Most: "I have at least two equal angles."

Some: "At least two of my sides are equal."

Few or no other: "I have three equal sides and three equal angles." (equilateral triangle)

Snowball

In Brief

Students reflect on their learning by writing a response to a question or topic the teacher poses.

*

Skills Practiced

Public speaking

Reasoning

Summarizing

Voicing an opinion

*

Time Frame

5–10 minutes

*

Materials

Slips of paper for each student

Chart paper or whiteboard (optional)

Pencils

*

Variation

Use this activity before teaching a new topic or unit to see what students already know or what they're most excited to learn.

HOW TO DO IT

1. **Name the learning goal.** For example: "You'll be reviewing the different themes in *The Wednesday Wars* by Gary Schmidt and how events in the novel relate to these themes."

2. **Ask a question or pose a topic for discussion:** "How does Holling's reading of Shakespeare's plays contribute to this novel's theme of friendship?" Students write their anonymous response on their paper.

3. **Everyone gathers in a standing circle (or remains at their desk),** crumples up their paper into a "snowball," and on your signal gently tosses it into the center (or into a bag).

4. **Tell students they'll carefully pick up a snowball** close to them (or out of the bag) and read aloud what's written on it. Remind them about effective communication skills: "What do you need to do when sharing so that everyone can hear you?"

5. **Go around the circle (or take turns)** and have everyone read their snowball out loud.

6. **Optional:** List all responses, grouping common ideas. Then hold a brief class discussion that reinforces positive behaviors and prompts further reflection: "I noticed a wide variety of responses and many different perspectives on this topic. What stood out to you as you listened to your classmates share?"

Learning Goal Examples

Math

"What's one thing you learned from our lesson on weekly budgets, and how might that affect your budgeting in real life?"

Related Arts (drama)

"What did you learn from putting on the play *Romeo and Juliet*, and how can you use that knowledge for our next play production?"

Snowball in Action

A teacher uses Snowball to help students recall and share test-taking strategies before mid-term exams. To direct students on the same path, he gives clear directions.

"We're going to think about strategies we use to stay focused when taking tests," he says, "and then we'll share our ideas with the class. Each person will think of a hint, tip, or strategy and write it on a piece of paper. Remember not to write your name down. After you finish writing, you're going to crumple up your paper to create a 'snowball.'"

Then he explains the timing and transitions: "Take two minutes to write your idea down. When you're finished, toss your snowball into the bag and return to your seat. Any questions before we get started?"

After everyone puts their snowball into the bag, the teacher picks them out, tossing one to each student. He gives them a chance to read their snowball silently before they read it aloud to the whole class. Afterward, he collects the snowballs and invites a few student volunteers to use them to create posters of the study tips for the whole class.

Learning Goal Examples

Science

"Name one energy source, where it comes from, and how we might use it more wisely."

Social Studies

"Write the most interesting fact you learned about daily life in ancient times."

Clock Partners

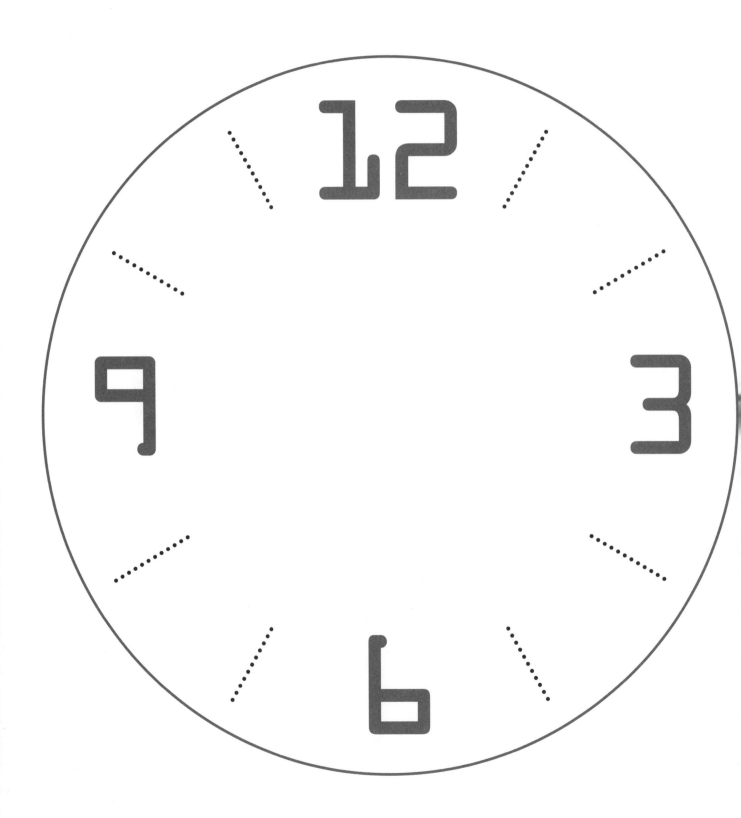

Consensus Map

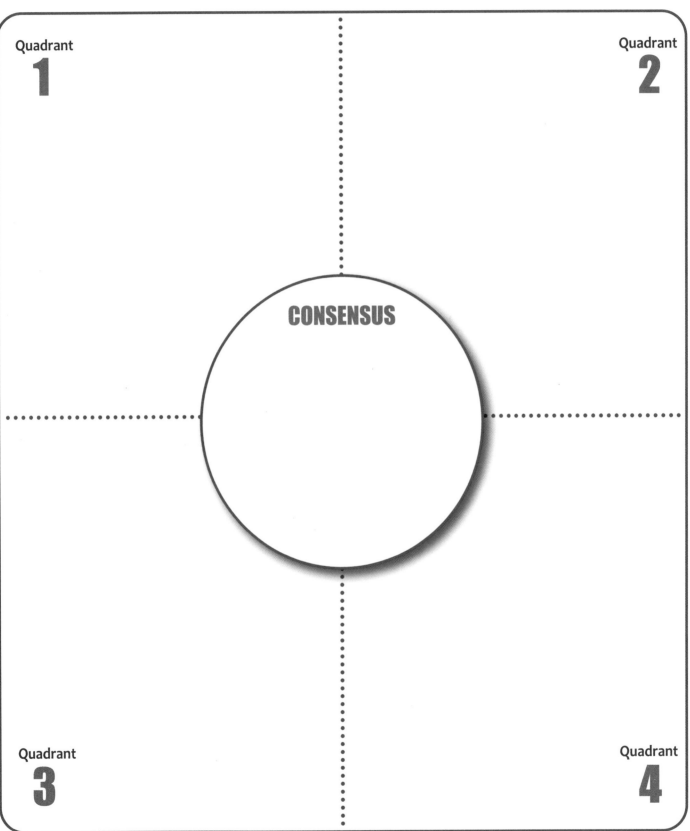

Quadrant
1

Quadrant
2

CONSENSUS

Quadrant
3

Quadrant
4

 **Debate Duos**

Topic: _____

Position A
(for): _____
_____

Position B
(against): _____
_____

Position A
Key Points: _____
_____
_____
_____
_____

Position B
Key Points: _____
_____
_____
_____
_____

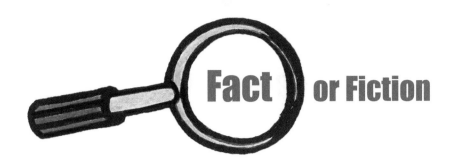

Fact or Fiction

Fact: _____

_____

_____

Fact: _____

_____

_____

Fiction: _____

_____

_____

Fact: _____

_____

_____

Fact: _____

_____

_____

Fiction: _____

_____

Jigsaws

Topic: _____

Expert Group Notes

Text/Audio/Video that my group focused on: _____

Key points we agreed on and will share with others: _____

_____

_____

Jigsaw Group Notes

Text/Audio/Video: _____   Text/Audio/Video: _____

Key points:_____   Key points:_____

_____   _____

_____   _____

Text/Audio/Video: _____   Text/Audio/Video: _____

Key points:_____   Key points:_____

_____   _____

_____   _____

Quiz Trade

Question: _____ | Answer: _____

_____ | _____

_____ | _____

_____ | _____

_____ | _____

Question: _____ | Answer: _____

_____ | _____

_____ | _____

_____ | _____

_____ | _____

Question: _____ | Answer: _____

_____ | _____

_____ | _____

_____ | _____

FOLD

Say Something

Title: _____

Resource: _____

Segment/Section 1: _____

Stop at: _____

Comments/Questions: _____

_____

_____

_____

_____

Segment/Section 2: _____

Stop at: _____

Comments/Questions: _____

_____

_____

_____

_____

Segment/Section 3: _____

Stop at: _____

Comments/Questions: _____

_____

_____

_____

_____

Segment/Section 4: _____

Stop at: _____

Comments/Questions: _____

_____

_____

_____

_____

Shared Truths

Topic: _____

True for most: _____

_____

_____

True for some: _____

_____

_____

e for just a few
or no other: _____

_____

_____

What I am: _____

Stay and Stray

Group:

Notes:

Group:

Notes:

Group:

Notes:

Swap Meet

Topic/Task: _____

My idea: _____

_____

_____

_____'s idea: _____

_____

_____

_____'s idea: _____

_____

_____

Summary of what I learned: _____

_____

_____

_____

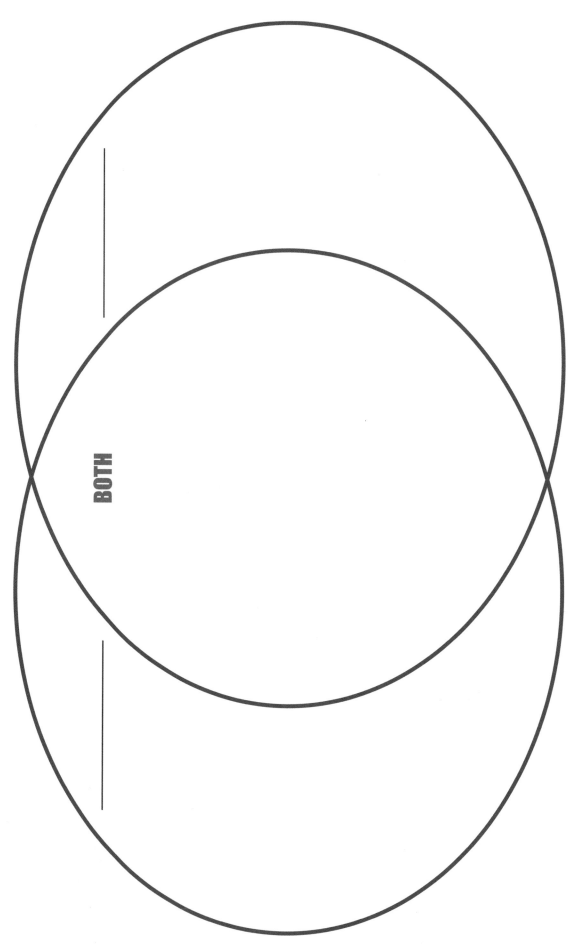

Venn-ting

BOTH

Middle School Motivators!   © 2016 Center for Responsive Schools, Inc. Permission to make personal copies is granted.

Word Splash

About the Publisher

Center for Responsive Schools, Inc., a not-for-profit educational organization, is the developer of *Responsive Classroom*®, a research-based education approach associated with greater teacher effectiveness, higher student achievement, and improved school climate. *Responsive Classroom* practices help educators build competencies in four inter-related domains: engaging academics, positive community, effective management, and developmentally responsive teaching. We offer the following resources for educators:

Professional Development Services

* Workshops for K–8 educators (locations around the country and internationally)

* On-site consulting services to support implementation

* Resources for site-based study

* Annual conferences for K–8 educators

Publications and Resources

* Books and videos

* Professional development kits for school-based study

* Free monthly newsletter

* Extensive library of free articles on our website

For details, contact:

Responsive Classroom®

Center for Responsive Schools, Inc.
85 Avenue A, P.O. Box 718
Turners Falls, Massachusetts 01376-0718

800-360-6332   www.responsiveclassroom.org
info@responsiveclassroom.org